Golf is usually played with the outward appearance of great dignity. It is, nevertheless, a game of considerable passion—either of the explosive type, or that which burns inwardly and sears the soul.

Robert Tyre Jones, Jr.

Augusta National, the 12th Hole

SOME OF US WORSHIP IN CHURCHES, SOME IN SYNAGOGUES, SOME ON GOLF COUR

A PASSION FOR

THE GAME OF GOLF

HUBERT PEDROLI
& MARY TIEGREEN

A Welcome Book
ANDREWS AND MCMEEL • KANSAS CITY

LAI STEVENSON

Why We Play Golf

July 1995. St. Andrews' Old Course. Constantino Rocca, a son of Italy and former factory worker, finds himself in a possible tie with U.S. champion John Daly on the final hole of the British Open. In a moment witnessed by tens of millions of TV viewers around the world, Rocca, facing the shot of a lifetime, foozles. The ball travels an embarrassing few feet downhill into the 18th hole's infamous "Valley of Sin." Curiously, agony is soon followed by ecstasy: Rocca, suddenly liberated from his golf demons, unleashes an aggressive putt from the far-distant fringe. Looking good from the start, the ball zooms across vast expanses of greenery toward its incredible rendezvous with destiny. At the end of a 65-foot journey, it vanishes into the hole, encompassing in one fateful event the entire magic of golf.

Indeed, while Constantino would go on to lose the championship in a play-off against Daly, history had once again witnessed a quintessential moment in golf. Under the solemn façade of the Royal and Ancient Clubhouse, golf humanity had fallen and risen again in the unending struggle between science and art, only to be redeemed by grace.

It is the like of such improbable antics that, for centuries now, has invigorated golf's faithful with uncompromising passion.

Constantino Rocca receives Golf's Amazing Grace at the 1995 British Open at St. Andrews.

TOM MORRIS
"The Grand Old Man of Golf" 1821–1908

Born in St. Andrews in 1821, Tom Morris learned his trade from golf professional Allan Robertson. He took charge of the links at Prestwick in 1851, but in 1865 he returned to his

Mr. Linskill has a trick of clearing his voice and booming the word "however," which has the effect of a wet rag wiped over a blackboard, clearing it for the next topic.

"Golf today," he said, "is a ladies' game compared with the golf I remember at St. Andrews half a century ago. I remember playing with hand-hammered gutta-percha balls. Damned annoying things when they broke! The rule in those days was that you put the new ball on the place where the largest fragment of the old one fell!

"I was taught by 'Young Tom' Morris.

The Old Course at St. Andrews is to golfers what the Vatican is to Catholics.
St. Andrews & Golf

By gad, sir, in those days the daisies were so thick at St. Andrews that we never played a white ball! I remember how the caddie used to say: 'Red or yellow ball, sir!' And, by Jove—the moonlight games! How dashed well I remember playing when the moon was full, with 'fore caddies to tell us where the ball had gone, and a fellow following behind with a wheelbarrow full of refreshments! Those were the days, my boy! However . . ."

H.V. Morton
In Search of Scotland, 1930

native town and became the Old Course's legendary greenskeeper. He won the British Open four times, and in his later years his grandfatherly image came to represent the Scottish game's venerable tradition and history.

Bobby Jones was the story. He was front-page news. For the six days of the U.S. Amateur, more than 2,200,000 words were written about Jones. Radio, officially celebrating its tenth anniversary, was giving national coverage to the championship. Every evening for fifteen minutes over NBC, O.B. Keeler would report a round-up from the Merion Cricket Club. On the Wednesday before the quarterfinals, Grantland Rice with the Coca-Cola Orchestra would devote a full half hour to the U.S. Amateur.

Richard Miller
Triumphant Journey

Matchless in skill and chivalrous in spirit, Bobby Jones lives forever as golfdom's most revered and cherished icon. Blessed with a graceful swing, a fearless determination, and a boyish smile, Jones captured 13 major titles in a period of 8 years. In his 1930 culminating triumph, Bobby, who had remained an amateur all along, won all four major championships: the British Amateur, the British Open, the U.S. Amateur, and the U.S. Open. Thereafter, he retired from the pressures of competitive golf at the ripe age of 28. But Bobby's contribution to the sport was far from over. In the following years, he would go on to design and build his ideal golf course, the famed Augusta National Golf Club; and in 1934, he presided over the inauguration of the Augusta National Invitational Tournament, later to become America's grand celebration of golf: "The Masters."

Jones was photographed wherever he went. Here he pauses for posterity after his British Amateur victory at St. Andrews in 1930, the first leg in his historic journey toward the "Impregnable Quadrilateral."

Golf encourages idleness, shiftlessness, and neglect of business as well as family responsibilities. It deprives many wives of their husbands and children of their fathers, and it tempts hundreds of young men into extravagance that sometimes leads to crime.

Mr. Quale, Federal Director of Prohibition Enforcement in Minnesota

RIGHT: Bobby Jones in a precarious position at the 1928 U.S. Amateur at Brae Burn Country Club, Newton, Massachusetts. Bobby won this match and later, the championship. ABOVE: The author (center) with friends two hours before his wedding.

Golf is a science, the study of a life time, in which you may exhaust yourself but never your subject. It is a contest, a duel or a melee, calling for courage, skill, strategy and self-control. ⚜ It is a test of temper, a trial of honour, a revealer of character. It affords a chance to play the man and act the gentleman. It means going into God's out-of-doors, getting close to nature, fresh air, exercise, a sweeping away of mental cobwebs, genuine recreation of tired tissues. It is a cure for care, an antidote to worry. It includes companionship with friends, social intercourse, opportunities for courtesy, kindliness and generosity to an opponent. It promotes not only physical health but moral force.

D.R. FORGAN, CLUB MAKER,
ST. ANDREWS, SCOTLAND

A man is standing on the tee ready to hit his drive. At that moment, a funeral procession passes by. The man steps back, takes off his hat and bows his head. After a moment of silence, his partner, surprised by the gesture, says:

"Bill, I never knew you were such a sensitive man!"

"It's the least I can do. We would have been married 35 years today."

The Elusive Hole-In-One

The average golfer, playing an average of 100 rounds a season on a course with four short holes, might expect to make a hole-in-one once every 23 years.

The odds against the average golfer getting a hole-in-one on a hole reachable in one shot are approximately 15,000 to 1.

There are two reasons for making a hole-in-one. The first is that it is immensely laborsaving.

H.I. Phillips, writer

Arnold Palmer had 16 holes-in-one in his career, including three at the second hole of his home course, Latrobe CC.

The 10th hole on Miracle Hill Golf Course in Omaha, Nebraska, was the scene of the longest hole-in-one to date. It was made by Bob Mitera, an American student, on October 7, 1965. The hole runs 477 yards.

The greatest number of holes-in-one achieved by an individual is 47 by Norman Manley of California.

PGA West Stadium Course's fearsome 17th hole island green left Lee Trevino unimpressed during the 1987 Skins Game. His 6-iron hole-in-one netted him $175,000.

The odds of making two holes-in-one in the same round are 500,000 to 1.

The earliest recorded hole-in-one was that of Young Tom Morris who, in 1868, aced the 8th hole at Prestwick during the Open Championship.

When asked his opinion on the most difficult shot in golf, Groucho Marx said, "I find it to be the hole-in-one."

A bottle of whisky was the traditional reward to the caddy for scoring a hole-in-one at either of the short holes at St. Andrews.

From the moment Hagen won his first British Open, his star lit up the golf sky and also cast a pretty bright glow over the entire Jazz Age. He was now "Sir Walter" or "The Haig," and he lived the role. He brought a noisy style to the golf wardrobe—alpaca sweaters, silk shirts, boisterous cravats, and argyle stockings that shouted attention for his black and white shoes for which he paid the unheard-of price of 100 dollars a pair. A handsome, five-foot ten-inch, 175 pounder, he wore

Walter Hagen with the Prince of Wales.

his jet black hair plastered to his skull. His drink in the Prohibition era of bathtub gin remained scotch and he consumed amounts that leveled many who tried to match him.

He traveled in chauffeured limousines. He golfed with the likes of the Emperor of Japan as well as the Prince of Wales and with American royalty like John D. Rockefeller.

Gerald Astor
The PGA World Golf Hall of Fame Book

I don't want to be a millionaire. I just want to live like one. *Walter Hagen*

Golf architecture is a new art closely allied to that of the artist or sculptor, but also necessitating a scientific knowledge of many other subjects.

In the old days, many golf courses were designed by prominent players who, after a preliminary inspection of the course, simply placed pegs to represent the suggested sites for the tees, greens and bunkers. The whole thing was completed in a few hours and the best results could hardly have been expected, and in fact never were obtained by these methods.

The modern designer, on the other hand, is likely to achieve the most perfect results and make the fullest use of the natural features by more up-to-date methods.

Alister MacKenzie
The Spirit of St. Andrews

Pete Dye

In the 1980's, Pete Dye revitalized golf course architecture. Inspired by the wooden "sleepers" that buttress Old Prestwick's fearsome bunkers, Dye transported the technique to America, and a new era in golf course design began. His trademark bulkheaded traps and water hazards delivered strikingly new visual contrasts on the course and brought a new meaning to the words "psychological warfare."

But Pete Dye was not done yet with his imaginative ploys. His controversial island green at the TPC at Sawgrass' 17th hole stimulated perhaps more criticism and imitation than any previous innovation in golf architecture. TV commentators soon popularized the expression "watery grave," and except for the pros, everyone loved it.

Pete Dye is seen here on the grounds of the future Ocean Course at Kiawah Island, S.C. The tough layout, which Dye was commissioned to build as the venue for the 1991 Ryder Cup matches, was the site of fierce individual battles. Its difficulty eventually galvanized the U.S. team to win a thin-margin victory over the foreign invaders.

ALTITUDES:

18   WORLD'S HIGHEST GOLF COURSE: Tuctu Golf Club, Peru, 14,335 feet.
     WORLD'S LOWEST GOLF COURSE: Kallia Golf Course, Jericho,
     1250 feet below sea level.

ARCHITECTS OF GOLF

Can you name the famous golf architects who designed the following masterpieces?

1. COURSE #2, PINEHURST CC, PINEHURST, NC
2. WINGED FOOT GC, MAMARONECK, NY
3. PINE VALLEY GC, NJ
4. HARBOUR TOWN GOLF LINKS, HILTON HEAD ISLAND, SC
5. NATIONAL GOLF LINKS OF AMERICA, SOUTHAMPTON, NY
6. CYPRESS POINT GC, PEBBLE BEACH, CA
7. SHADOW CREEK GOLF CLUB, LAS VEGAS, NV
8. SPYGLASS HILL GC, PEBBLE BEACH, CA
9. THE PRINCE GOLF COURSE, PRINCEVILLE, HI
10. DESERT HIGHLANDS, SCOTTSDALE, AZ

Answers can be found on page 21.

THE 17TH HOLE AT PGA WEST STADIUM COURSE
Pete Dye's replay of his Sawgrass classic island hole has become a classic itself. The impregnable fortress, "Alcatraz," sits in the middle of a lake, flanked by ragged-edged boulders to deflect any unwelcome projectiles.

Considering that Shadow Creek was artificially created in a corner of the desert outside Las Vegas, its number 8 ranking in *Golf Digest* America's 100 Greatest Courses was an outstanding inauguration. Casino owner Steve Wynn spared nothing to fulfill his dream. To design the layout, Wynn recruited famed architect Tom Fazio and gave him a blank check. Mountains of rock and sand were moved, thousands of mature pines were transplanted onto the site, and, on the sixth day, a string of streams and lakes was excavated to bring life to this "Biosphere of Golf." A few months and $37 million later, a new corner of paradise had been created.

Shadow Creek
Shadow Creek Golf Club, Las Vegas.
Designed by Tom Fazio, assisted by
owner Steve Wynn.

The greatest compliment that can be paid to the architect is for players to think that his artificial work is natural.
Alister MacKenzie, *Golf Architecture*, 1920

ANSWERS: 1. Donald Ross
2. A.W. Tillinghast
3. G. Crump with H.S. Colt
4. Pete Dye with Jack Nicklaus
5. C.B. MacDonald
6. Alister MacKenzie
7. Tom Fazio
8. Robert Trent Jones
9. Robert Trent Jones, Jr.
10. Jack Nicklaus

21

On a golf-hole-per-square-mile basis, Myrtle Beach is far and away the springtime golf capital of eastern North America. There are something like eighty courses on the strip of Carolina seaside known as the Grand Strand, and so many more are under construction that the maps on the placemats in the restaurants are invariably out of date. During the peak spring season—which runs roughly from the middle of March until the first of June—the area fills with men from the North whose veins are throbbing with resurgent golf hormones. During the two months before our late-February departure date, I remembered what it felt like to be a child waiting for Christmas. By the time the great day arrived, my partners and I were so excited that we could scarcely make intelligent conversation with our wives, who were no longer speaking to us anyway.

David Owen
My Usual Game

Motel golf packages available

Myrtle Beach, South Carolina
Golf Capital of the Universe

Web Site: http://www.myrtlebeach-info.com/golf/golf.html

Golf Courses: 86
Soon to be 100

**Golf Course
Architects
Represented:**
Jack Nicklaus
Tom Fazio
Pete Dye
P.B. Dye
Dan Maples
Arnold Palmer
Robert Trent Jones
Rees Jones
Gary Player
Arthur Hills
Tom Doak
Willard Byrd
Raymond Floyd
and more . . .

**Miniature Golf
Courses:** 13
Involving Pirates: 5

Restaurants:
Seafood: 25
Steak Houses: 12
Serving grits: 852

**Average Golfing
Weather:**
Spring: Perfect
Summer: Balmy
Fall: Delicious
Winter: Cheap

Accommodations:
Number of
Hotels/Motels: 250

Number of
Hotels/Motels
whose name
starts with:
Sand: 6
(including Sand Castle)
Ocean: 14
Tropical: 5
Beach: 5
(including Beachcomber)
Sea: 13
Driftwood: 1
Polynesian: 1

Whatta Gal! The Story of the Babe

A champion in every sport she tried, she was the finest athlete the twentieth century would know. An outstanding performer in the 1932 Olympics, Mildred "Babe" Didrickson set new records in javelin and hurdles, and was on her way to a gold medal in the high jump when she was disqualified for jumping over the bar head first! Basketball, swimming, diving, softball, and tennis held no secrets for her, but it was through golf that the Babe acquired her fame. She was the first American woman to win the British Championship, and she went on to win three U.S. Opens. Her straight-forward approach to people and golf is best illustrated by her answer when asked how she could drive the ball such tremen-dous distances: "Well, I just loosen my girdle and let the ball have it."

A BRIEF HISTORY OF THE GOLF BALL

THE FEATHERIE

The "Featherie" (found in use as early as the 1400's) was made of a leather wrapping stuffed with a top hat full of boiled goose feathers. It was expensive, lost its shape quickly, and its performance would be seriously affected by a bout of inclement Scottish weather. A drive with the Feather Ball would average 175-to 200-yards,

but a 361-yard monster by Mr. Samuel Messieux was officially recorded on St. Andrews' Elysian Fields in 1836, testimony to the unpredictable but occasionally spirited character of the venerable Featherie.

THE GUTTA-PERCHA

Around 1850, the "Gutta-Percha" ball appeared. Made of molten tree-sap, it should have been no threat to the Feather Ball. Its record drives of 175 yards were sometimes shorter than the Featherie's, and it would break into pieces at the most inopportune times. But considerably less expensive to manufacture and more durable (it could be remolded), the "Guttie" soon replaced the

Featherie on the links as thousands of new pilgrims joined the golf religion.

THE HASKELL BALL

At the turn of the century, the rubber-core ball (also known as "The Haskell") appeared on the scene. It carried and rolled 25 yards further than the Guttie, and was quickly adopted by golfers as their preferred predicament off the tee and on the greens. More distance and consistency meant a real breakthrough for the game. A few of the old courses were rendered too short by the invention, but the ball's added liveliness also led golfers to discover theretofore unexplored confines of the rough.

DISCLAIMER: Due to the unreliability of golfers' accounts of their driving distances, this chart is for illustration purposes only.

OOMPH!

THE MODERN BALL

Ultimate salvation was finally in sight when the Modern Ball era began in the 1930s. Experimenting with such diverse and exotic compounds as tapioca, honey, balata, and polybutadiene, ball makers created 2-piece or 3-piece projectiles that finally delivered astounding distance and pinpoint accuracy, with a durability well in excess of the ball's life expectancy between water hazards.

Then came the USGA, and for millions, the end of a dream. The Modern Golf World's Ruling Body capped a golf ball's maximum velocity at 250 feet per second and its maximum distance at 296.8 yards.

Thus Mr. Messieux of St. Andrews could finally rest in peace, secure in the knowledge that his famous Featherie record would not suffer the insult of being trampled daily by millions of mediocre golfers all over the world.

GOOD NEWS FOR GOLF INSOMNIACS:

Restless golfers need no longer spend sleepless nights counting St. Andrews' sheep jumping over the fence between the Old and the New Course. Thanks to modern technology, night golf is here. Teeing off with glow-in-the-dark balls, golfers can now indulge in their favorite pastime 24 hours a day, including during the wee hours previously reserved for indoor sports.

THE MODERN BALL

THE HASKELL BALL

FEATHERIE

GUTTA-PERCHA

296.8 YARDS

> If profanity had any influence on the flight of the ball, the game would be played far better than it is.
>
> Horace G. Hutchinson, golf historian

THE PAR-AIDE STORY
A familiar silhouette on golf courses all over the planet, the Par-Aide ball washer was invented in 1954 by Joseph Garske. His spiraling agitator, which he patented in 1957, met with little interest when offered for $25,000 to already established companies. Soon, Joseph Garske was in the golf business himself and the Par-Aide company was founded. Another symbol of American ingenuity and cultural influence in the modern world.

ODE TO THE BALL WASHER

by Lance Nordstrom, D.D.S.

f many tee-shot horrors a silent witness,
The Ball Washer discretion does possess.
Air-shots and worm-burners, a thousand has he seen,
Yet of the dirty deeds, no blabbermouth has been.

We grab him by the head, in fits of agitation,
But a shiny ball he spits, with no word of protestation.
Standing for decades at the Offenders' service,
This quiet little man we can no longer dismiss.

Dressed in mere towels, yet noble and correct,
It's time for the Par-Aide man to get his due respect.
His silent, steely gaze keeps Mulligans in check,
For they can feel his stare when they reload on deck.

Were it not for him, more than balls would be dirty;
For the cheaters' conscience Par-Aide man keeps tidy.

TEMPORARY RULES, 1941
Richmond Golf Club · London, England

1. Players are asked to collect the bomb and shrapnel splinters to save these causing damage to the mowing machines.

2. In competitions, during gunfire or while bombs are falling, players may take shelter without penalty for ceasing play.

3. The positions of known delayed action bombs are marked by red flags at a reasonable, but not guaranteed, safe distance therefrom.

4. Shrapnel and/or bomb splinters on the Fairways, or in Bunkers, within a club's length of a ball, may be moved without penalty, and no penalty shall be incurred if a ball is thereby caused to move accidentally.

5. A ball moved by enemy action may be replaced, or if lost, or destroyed, a ball may be dropped no nearer the hole without penalty.

6. A ball lying in a crater may be lifted and dropped not nearer the hole, preserving the line to the hole, without penalty.

7. A player whose stroke is affected by the simultaneous explosion of a bomb may play another ball. Penalty one stroke.

Golf, in fact, is the only game in the world in which a precise knowledge of the rules can earn one a reputation for bad sportsmanship.

Patrick Campbell,
golf instructor

WORLD CLASS BUNKERS

The following ten "sandy graves" are located on courses in the British Isles and in the U.S. Can you name their locations?

1. SAN ANDREAS FAULT

2. THE THREE SISTERS

3. THE DEVIL'S ASSHOLE

4. THE CHURCH PEWS

5. THE SPECTACLES

6. THE ROAD HOLE BUNKER

7. THE PRINCIPAL'S NOSE

8. THE CARDINAL

9. HELL'S HALF ACRE

10. THE COFFINS

Answers can be found on pages 32–33.

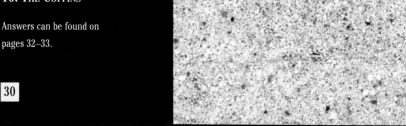

Greg Norman demonstrates his touch while blasting out of trouble.

Over time, the most infamous bunkers have acquired names that send shivers of fear down the strained spines of the golfing faithful. The Old Course possesses perhaps the best-known collection of renegades, starting with Hell Bunker, which trapped and chewed up the Golden Bear himself during the first round of the 1995 British Open. He escaped with his life, and a 10 for the hole.

Surprisingly, the bunker shot is actually considered by many to be easier than a chip from the rough. Here are some simple instructions to get out of the sand:

STEP 1: Address the shot with your weight on the left foot and your hands well ahead of the clubface.

STEP 2: Pick a spot 3 inches behind the ball. This is where the blade will enter the sand.

STEP 3: Take the club back smoothly while keeping your head still.

STEP 4: Hit down and through, always keeping your hands ahead of the clubface.

STEP 5: Finish high with a winning smile.

Repeat steps 2 through 5 as needed until desired result is achieved. If symptoms persist, consult a swing doctor immediately.

$\mathcal{B}$unkers, if they are good bunkers, and bunkers of strong character, refuse to be disregarded and insist on asserting themselves. They do not mind being avoided, but they decline to be ignored.

Architect John Low
Concerning Golf, 1903

THE DEVIL'S ASSHOLE BUNKER HOLE #10, PINE VALLEY

The pot bunker on Pine Valley's 10th hole is rude even with the members. They often prefer to hit a second ball rather than deal with the Devil's anatomy.

Scotland. 6. Hole #17, St. Andrews Old Course, Scotland. 7. Hole #16, St. Andrews Old Course.

8. Hole #3, Prestwick, Scotland. 9. Hole #7, Pine Valley GC, NJ. 10. Hole #13, St. Andrews Old Course.

33

A Different Game

eople talk about Couples playing a fade, or working the ball from left to right, but his fades don't look anything like the shots that you and I refer to as fades. They are not miniature slices. A trademark Couples drive takes off dead straight and rising at what seems like the speed of sound. About 250 yards out, it levels off and bends perhaps one degree to the right. It returns to earth at roughly the 300-yard mark, and rolls another twenty or thirty yards down the middle of the fairway. It is not a banana.

David Owen
My Usual Game

Fred Couples displays his effortless swing getting out of a bunker.

ON PUTTING

The devoted golfer is an anguished soul who has learned a lot about putting, just as an avalanche victim has learned a lot about snow. He knows he has used putters with straight shafts, curved shafts, shiny shafts, dull shafts, glass shafts, oak shafts and Great-uncle Clyde's World War I saber, which he found in the attic. Attached to these shafts have been putter heads made of large lumps of lead ("weight makes the ball roll true," salesmen explain) and slivers of aluminum ("lightness makes the ball roll true," salesmen explain) as well as every other substance harder than a marshmallow. He knows he has tried forty-one different stances, inspired by everyone from the club pro to Fred Astaire in *Flying Down to Rio*, and just as many different strokes. Still, he knows, he is hopelessly trapped. He can't putt, and he never will, and the only thing left for him to do is bury his head in the dirt and live the rest of his life like a radish.

Dan Jenkins
The Dogged Victims of Inexorable Fate

Why am I using a new putter? Because the old one didn't float too well.

*Craig Stadler,
at the 1993 U.S. Open*

Goldfinger was practicing on the putting green. His caddie stood nearby, rolling balls to him. Goldfinger putted in the new fashion—between his legs with a mallet putter. Bond felt encouraged. He didn't believe in the system. He knew it was no good practicing himself. His old hickory Calamity Jane had its good days and its bad. There was nothing to do about it.

Ian Fleming
Goldfinger

He holed his short putt and the next instant there was no green visible, only a dark seething mass, in the midst of which was Bobby hoisted on fervent shoulders and holding his putter, "Calamity Jane" at arms' length over his head, lest she be crushed to death. Calamity Jane had two pieces of whipping bound round her shaft where she had been broken, not we may trust in anger, but by some mischance. When, some years later, the market was flooded with exact models of her, each of them duly bore two superfluous black bands. Did ever imitation pay sincerer flattery than that?

Bernard Darwin
Golf Between Two Wars

There is no similarity between golf and putting; they are two different games. One is played in the air and the other on the ground.

Ben Hogan

Few pleasures on earth match the feeling that comes from making a loud bodily-function noise just as a guy is about to putt.

Dave Barry, humorist

Golfing great Sam Snead won over 135 tournaments in his forty-year career. However, his admirable ability with the driver was often betrayed by a fickle putting blade. He is seen here taking no chances with a slippery three-footer.

If I had to choose between my wife and my putter, well, I'd miss her.

Gary Player, on the putter he's used since 1967

Ninety percent of putts that are short don't go in.

Yogi Berra

1991 RYDER CUP MATCHES, KIAWAH ISLAND
European team veteran Bernhard Langer misses a crucial
6-footer on the 18th hole of the Ocean Course. The U.S. team
clinched a narrow victory over the visitors, thus regaining
possession of the cup for the first time since 1983.

39

The man who revolutionized golf

Science and engineering were Karsten Solheim's first passions. In fact, his creative mind was behind the invention of a ubiquitous ornament of most 1970's American family rooms and dens: the TV "rabbit ears." (No, he did not invent aluminum foil.) So, it was not until the age of 43 that Karsten played his first round of golf. His initial experiences with the game were not unlike most beginners', but it was on the putting green that the Norwegian-born mastermind encountered his greatest frustration. No human physical limitation could account for the blade's temperamental performance, he reasoned, and soon Karsten had his revelation: *"If it were not the puttee, it had to be the putter."* Karsten hurried back to his shop and by dinner time he had a new, albeit odd-looking, weapon: two thin metal blades bridging two cylindrical masses. Karsten dropped a ball on the dining room carpet, hit it, and the ball rolled true into the glass. "Heel-toe weighting" had been invented and a strange new sound had been added to golf's grand symphony.

LEFT: Karsten Solheim and the blueprints of his revolutionary putter. ABOVE: Karsten's best-selling Ping Anser putter.

Total Victories: 92
PGA Tour Victories: 61
PGA Senior Tour: 12
1954 U.S. Amateur Champion
"Major" Titles:
    1958 Masters
    1960 Masters
    1960 U.S. Open
    1961 British Open
    1962 Masters
    1962 British Open
    1964 Masters

Special Achievements
    PGA Player of the Year:
      1960 & 1962
    PGA Tour leading money winner:
      1958, 1962, 1964, 1967
    Vardon Trophy Winner:
      1961, 1962, 1964, 1967
    Ryder Cup Team: 1961, 1963,
      1965, 1967, 1971, 1973
      (Captain 1963, 1975)
    Chrysler Cup Team & Captain:
      1966 through 1990
    Best 18-hole round in a
      tournament: 62
    All-time low 18-hole score:
      60, Latrobe CC

Arnold Palmer

Arnold Palmer's game was never short on panache and valor, but his 92 professional victories, including 7 Majors, reflect only part of the legend's widespread achievements. Jet-aircraft pilot, businessman, golf architect, and ambassador of goodwill, the "King's" gallant approach to golf and life has won him the hearts of millions of fans in the world. To this day, a round of golf with "Arnie" remains the average golfing man's most cherished dream.

The most rewarding things you do in life are often the ones that look like they can't be done.

Arnold Palmer

I had always suspected that trying to play golf in the company of big time pros and a gallery would be something like walking naked into choir practice. And it was. In that moment on the 1st tee, I suddenly felt blinded and flushed, and that I would like to be somewhere else. Bolivia, maybe.

As I bent over to tee up the ball, I could barely see my hand shaking. I remember being able to taste a giant cotton rabbit in my mouth as I addressed the shot. I remember catching a glimpse of my shoes and wishing they had been shined. And I remember that as I took the club back, I overheard another comment in the gallery.

"No livin' way," a man said, quietly.

The drive went somewhere down the fairway, rather remarkably, but the next shot went only fifteen or twenty feet. I topped it. The next one went about ten yards. I topped it again. And the next one went about fifty yards. I hit a foot behind it. Eventually, I managed to pitch onto the putting surface, a feat that was greeted with a ripple of applause, which I took for what it was: a slightly unnecessary sarcasm from a few of my own friends in the crowd.

For a moment or so, I felt all right. I was on the green at last where I could stand around with Arnold and Dow, lean casually on my putter, and smoke. Except when I walked onto the lovely bent grass, I accidentally dragged one foot and my cleats carved a horrible divot out of the turf.

Humiliated, naturally, I quickly got down on my hands and knees to repair the divot. But when I got back up I noticed that the moisture of the green had implanted a huge damp splotch on each knee of my trousers. I leaned over and stared at the

ARNOLD PALMER AND DOW FINSTERWALD

splotches, and began to give each leg a casual ruffle. When I raised up, my head hit something hard. It was my caddy's chin. He had come over to hand me the putter.

I took the putter and went over to my ball. I marked it and tried to hand it to the caddy so he could clean it. I dropped it. We both bent over to pick it up, bumped shoulders, and then got our hands on it at the same time. I dropped my putter. He dropped the towel. I picked up the towel. He picked up the putter. We exchanged them.

At this point, I thought I would light a cigarette to steady the nerves. I removed the pack from my pocket and tapped it against my left hand the way one does to make the cigarettes pop out. About four of them squirted out and onto the green. I picked them up and lit one. But when I went to remove it from my dry lips, it stuck, my fingers slid off the end, knocking the burning head down onto my shirt front. This forced me into a bit of an impromptu dance, which in turn, resulted in my cleats taking another huge divot out of the green.

When that divot had been repaired, when I had successfully lighted another cigarette, and when I had a firm grip on the putter, I glanced around to see where Palmer and Finsterwald were and realized they had been staring at me, along with the other amused thousands, for God knows how long. It had been my turn to putt.

Dan Jenkins
The Dogged Victims of Inexorable Fate

Bob Hope's swing? I've seen better swings on a condemned playground. *Bing Crosby*

BOB HOPE ON GOLF

I'd give up golf if I didn't have so many sweaters.

I didn't realize how long some of these seniors have been around. Yesterday I saw a guy signing his scorecard with a feather.

Some of these legends have been around golf a long time. When they mention a good grip, they're talking about their dentures.

I get upset over a bad shot just like anyone else. But it's silly to let the game get to you. When I miss a shot I just think what a beautiful day it is. And what pure fresh air I'm breathing. Then I take a deep breath. I have to do that. That's what gives me the strength to break the club.

Babe liked to play to the audience. We did many exhibitions together. On a par-3 hole, if I hit first, she'd ask me, "What club did you use, Bob?" I'd say a 4-iron. In a loud voice that the gallery couldn't miss, she'd laugh and tell her caddie, "Give me an 8-iron."

But it was a great day, even though Jack's course is so difficult. I had a 9 on the 1st hole before I got it out of the ball washer.

A few years ago Arnold went on a fitness program. He started jogging and gave up smoking. And he looks great.

He coughs only when his opponent is putting.

Whenever I play with Gerald Ford, I try to make it a foursome—the President, myself, a paramedic, and a faith healer.

Arnie's really had a fabulous career in golf. He's won as much money as I've spent on lessons. He told me how I could cut eight strokes off my score . . . skip one of the par 3s.

The last time we played, Arnold was only a couple of strokes up on me. Then we went on to the 2nd hole.

For some reason, many amateurs like to give free advice, or solicit free tips from the pro. The pros hear "What am I doing wrong?" more times than Dolores did on our honeymoon.

On Billy Graham: I sank a 35-foot putt against him, turned around and my caddie had turned into a pillar of salt.

When I first heard about the Skins Game, I expected to see a match between Telly Savalas, Don Rickles and Alan Cranston. The Skins Game . . . it sounds like golf at a nudist camp.

Player made $150,000 on one hole. I get goose bumps when I find a dime that someone's left in a pay phone.

But I digress. It's time to head over to Lakeside for

another round of golf. I know I'll shoot a good score because now I'm using an orthopedic putter. I'm shooting my age consistently these days, but nobody believes I'm 108.

Inseparable partners on the silver screen and on the golf course, Bob Hope and Bing Crosby are both members of the World Golf Hall of Fame. The success of their namesake tournaments is an enduring testimony to their passion for the game of golf.

Joyce Wethered and Glenna Collett Vare were great competitors throughout the 1920s. Joyce Wethered is seen here in California in 1935.

great champions have an enormous sense of pride. The people who excel are those who are driven to show the world—and prove to themselves— just how good they are.

Nancy Lopez

GLENNA COLLETT VARE
They called her "the Bobby Jones of women's golf." The best woman golfer of the 1920's, she is seen here (right) approaching the sixth hole at Pebble Beach. In all, she won the U.S. Women's Championship a record six times.

Nancy Lopez

Nancy was the champion the LPGA and the fans had been waiting for. Young, athletic, blessed with a sunny smile and warm personality, she burst onto the women's professional golf scene in 1978. By the end of her memorable first year she had won nine tournaments, setting a new money-winning record and becoming the first pro golfer ever to win both the "Player of the Year" and "Rookie of the Year" awards in the same season. Having recorded 35 professional victories, including two LPGA Championships, Nancy Lopez earned her spot in the LPGA Hall of Fame in 1989, long after she had won her special place in the hearts of her fans.

Marion Hollins

Born to a wealthy Long Island family in 1893, Marion Hollins was an accomplished golfer and early defender of women's causes. In 1921, she won the Women's Amateur Championship and went on to challenge men on their own turf. An entrepreneur as much as an activist, she energized the creation of the first all-woman golf club, and was the first woman to enter in an automobile race. After she fell in love with California's Monterey Peninsula, she and her partners created Pasatiempo Country Club & Estates in 1928, and recruited Alister MacKenzie to design the course. The grand opening match, held in 1929, featured an all-star foursome with guests Glenna Collett, Bobby Jones, and British champion Cyril Tolley. It is perhaps during that visit that Bobby Jones met Alister MacKenzie for the first time. In 1930, Marion Hollins's exploration partnership struck oil and she became a millionaire. She spent the rest of her life entertaining celebrities at her beloved Pasatiempo resort, having secured a little-known but highly significant place in golf history.

What Bing Crosby and Bob Hope did for the the PGA Tour, Dinah Shore (below) did for the LPGA. Her tournament, the Colgate–Dinah Shore Winner's Circle, started in 1972, and ten years later it had become one of the major tournaments on the ladies' tour. Today, the championship, now called The Nabisco Dinah Shore, continues to attract the best players and most popular celebrities.

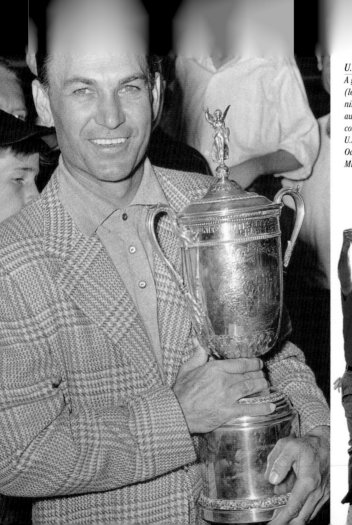

U.S. OPEN CHAMPIONSHIP
A great among greats, Ben Hogan (left) came back to win six of his nine major titles after a terrible automobile accident that almost cost him his life. One of his four U.S. Open victories came here at Oakland Hills CC, Birmingham, Michigan, in 1951.

Curtis Strange (left) one of the few champ to win back-to-back U Opens (1988 and 198

U.S WOMEN'S OPEN CHAMPIONSHIP

Mickey Wright holds the U.S. Women's Open trophy at Baltusrol in 1961. During her career, she won nearly 80 professional tournaments, including four U.S. Opens and four LPGA Championships.

RYDER CUP MATCHES

Ben Hogan (center) was the captain of the 1949 U.S. Ryder Cup team. Except for the year 1957, the U.S. side remained undefeated in the Ryder Cup matches from 1935 to 1985. Since then, ownership of the cup has been hotly disputed between Europe and the U.S. Pictured above are (l to r): Dutch Harrison, Johnny Palmer, Bob Hamilton, Sam Snead, Ben Hogan (non-playing Captain), Clayton Heafner, Jimmy Demaret, Lloyd Mangrum, and Chick Harbert.

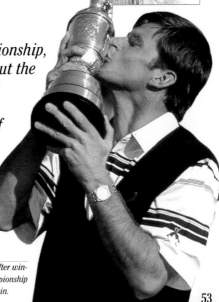

In a major championship, you don't care about the money. You're just trying to get your name on a piece of silver—that's all you're trying to do.

Nick Faldo

THE BRITISH OPEN

Nick Faldo kisses the Claret Jug after winning the 1990 British Open Championship with an authoritative 5-shot margin.

53

Let us pray . . .

Site of many a Sunday afternoon drama,
"Amen Corner" is perhaps the most revered
and recognized theatre in all of golf. In the
short stretch of three holes, 11th, 12th, and
13th, Jones and MacKenzie were able to incor-
porate all three classic styles of golf architecture and combine them in the most memorable display of challenge and beauty. The
downhill 11th, with its slick green fronted by a
menacing pond, demands a strategically
placed tee-shot. Then to the 12th, the familiar
155-yard devil over Rae's Creek; its shallow
putting surface and fierce bunkering make it
the most penal hole of the Masters and the
spectators' favorite. And finally the par-5 13th,
where Rae's Creek's meandering charms lure
the players into admirable acts of heroism.

*Augusta's 485-yard par-5 13th offers a great birdie opportunity. But
Rae's Creek, in front of the green, remains the ultimate judge of a
player's approach.*

54

You're only here
for a short visit.
Don't hurry.
Don't worry.
And be sure to
smell the flowers
along the way.

Walter Hagen

SEVE BALLESTEROS
ENJOYING THE AZALEAS . . .
Seve Ballesteros paid proper tribute to
Augusta's celebrated blooms during the 1984
Masters. Known for his heroic recoveries,
the Spanish champion safely escaped from
the flowery jail with a six-iron, positioning
himself for a fine third shot to the treacher-
ous 13th green.

Jack Nicklaus

Comparing performances in a centuries old sport is a delicate craft. Thankfully, it need not be attempted when looking at Jack Nicklaus's record. Jack **is** the greatest golfer that ever lived. He won his first official tournament, the Ohio State Juniors, at age 13 and his first U.S. Amateur at age 19, thus becoming the youngest U.S. Amateur champion in 50 years. In 1960, he came knocking on Arnold Palmer's door when he was a runner-up at the U.S. Open at Cherry Hills. Two years later he defeated the reigning king of golf in a heated Open playoff at Oakmont, and in 1963 the

king himself bestowed the Master's jacket on the young champion's shoulders. It was Jack's first green coat, but it would not be his last. Arnie struck back at Augusta in

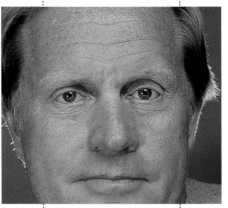

1964 and was able to reclaim his crown momentarily, but Jack ended the argument in 1965 and again in 1966, becoming the first champion to successfully defend his Master's title. In the 1970's,

the guard changed, but the Golden Bear did not notice. Fighting the likes of Gary Player, Lee Trevino, Johnny Miller, and soon Tom Watson, his claws were never far behind on the leaderboard. In all, Nicklaus would win eight major titles between 1970 and 1979 and he was runner-up six times! In 1980, the Golden Bear celebrated the beginning of his third decade of professional golf by winning the U.S. Open at Baltusrol, but when Watson clinched away from his paws the Open title in the fateful 1982 Pebble Beach encounter, many thought that Jack's extraordinary stretch in the majors had finally ended. "Never wake up a sleeping bear!" Lee Trevino had warned us a long time before. In April of 1986, Jack was out of hibernation and haunting his favorite grounds again: The Augusta National. On Sunday afternoon, the clamoring crowds could be heard among the pines and blooming azaleas; and, when the thundering applause finally ceased on the 18th fairway and his last putt had been holed, the world of golf could once again stand up, throw its arms up in the air, and shout out joyfully: *"Yes! Jack is back!"*

Another birdie putt rolls in for the Golden Bear during his incredible 1986 Masters comeback.

Jack is playing an entirely different game —a game I am not even familiar with.

Bobby Jones on Jack Nicklaus, 1965

The essence of the man might well have been that he embodied the spirit of golf more than anyone who ever played the game.

Jack Nicklaus on Bobby Jones, 1995

Credits

For information write:
Andrews and McMeel
A Universal Press Syndicate Company
4900 Main Street
Kansas City, Missouri 64112

PHOTOGRAPHY:

Photographs appearing on pages 2, 4, 17, 18, 21, 31, 33, 35, 38, 40, 43, 52 (Curtis Strange), 53 (Nick Faldo), 55, 56, 57, 58, and 64 courtesy of Jim Moriarty. Photographs appearing on pages 8, 9, 10–11, 14, 15, 24, 25, 37, 42, 47, 48, 49, 50, 51, 52 (Ben Hogan), 53 (Ryder Cup Team; Mickey Wright), and 60–61 courtesy of the Ralph Miller Golf Library/Museum. Page 37: photo of Sam Snead AP/Wide World Photos. Various golf ephemera from the Tiegreen/Pedroli Collection.

EDITORIAL:

Page 6–7: From "In Search of Scotland" by H. V. Morton. Copyright © 1929, 1930 by H.V. Morton. Published by Dodd, Mead and Company, 1930. • Page 8: From "Triumphant Journey" by Richard MIller. Copyright © 1980 by Dick Miller. Reprinted by permission of Taylor Publishing Company, Dallas, TX. • Page 14: From "The PGA World Golf Hall of Fame Book" by Gerald Astor. Copyright © 1991 by The PGA World Golf Hall of Fame, Inc. and Gerald Astor. Reprinted by permission of Prentice Hall Press. • Page 16: From "The Spirit of St. Andrews" by Alister MacKenzie. Copyright © 1995 Raymund M. Haddock. Reprinted by permission of Sleeping Bear Press, Chelsea, MI. • Pages 22 and 34: From "My Usual Game" by David Owen. Copyright © 1995 by David Owen. Reprinted by permission of Villard Books, a division of Random House. • Page 28: From "In Praise of Ordinary Things: Volume 2: Outdoor Things" by Lance Nordstrom, D.D.S. Copyright © 1962, by Lance Nordstrom. Reprinted by permission of The Nordstrom Press. • Pages 34 and 44–45: From "The Dogged Victims of Inexorable Fate" by Dan Jenkins. Copyright © 1970 by Dan Jenkins. Reprinted by permission of Little, Brown, and Company. • Page 36: From "Goldfinger" by Ian Fleming. Copyright © 1959 by Glidrose Publications Ltd. Reprinted by permission of Glidrose Publications Ltd. • Page 46:

From "Bob Hope's Confessions of a Hooker, My Lifelong Love Affair with Golf" by Bob Hope as told to Dwayne Netland. Copyright © 1985, 1987 by Bob Hope. Reprinted by permission of Doubleday & Company, Inc.

NOTE: Every effort has been made to locate the copyright owners of the material used in this book. Please let us know if an error has been made, and we will make any necessary corrections in subsequent printings.

A Welcome Book
WELCOME ENTERPRISES, INC.
575 Broadway
New York, New York 10012
Design by
Mary Tiegreen
Library of Congress Catalog Card Number: 95-80757
ISBN: 0-8362-1328-9

Printed in China by Toppan Printing

2 4 6 8 10 9 7 5 3 1

Acknowledgments

We would like to express our thanks to the following individuals and entities:

To Hiro Clark (left) of Welcome Enterprises for entrusting us with the responsibility of creating this essay on the Royal and Ancient game, and for allowing us the editorial freedom required to properly address the elusive and complex nature of our subject;

To the Ralph W. Miller Golf Library and Museum, City of Industry, California, for opening its large collection of golf books and images to our research, and especially to Marge Dewey and Saundra Sheffer, its dedicated Golf Librarians, for their patience and interest in sharing with us their formidable knowledge of the game's history and written record;

To Jim Moriarty, for making available to us his extensive portfolio of fine golf photographs, and for graciously sharing with us his knowledge of the links;

And to Daisy, our Golden Retriever (shown here at the TPC at Scottsdale), for preserving the confidentiality of our project by shredding any documents that may have mistakenly escaped our attention.

(Following page) Arnold Palmer's farewell to the British Open at St. Andrews, 1995.

Thank God for the game of golf.
Arnold Palmer